DISCOVER THE POWER OF YOUR EMOTIONS

Discover the Power of Your Emotions

Snehal Jain

Copyright © 2025 by Snehal Jain
All rights reserved. No part of this book may be reproduced in any manner whatsoever without written permission except in the case of brief quotations embodied in critical articles and reviews.
First Printing, 2025

Contents

Dedication — vi
Acknowledgement — vii
Preface — viii
Foreword — ix
Book Review — x

1. My Journey — 1
2. Don't Let Love Blind you — 5
3. Building Dreams Against All Odds — 8
4. Unlock the Strength from Within — 10
5. Resilience in the Face of Adversity — 14
6. Despair to Discovery — 17
7. Why Me? Karma and Fate — 20
8. Forgiveness: A Path to Spiritual Liberation — 23
9. The Mirror Effect: Harnessing the Power Within — 25
10. Harnessing the Energy of Abundance — 28
11. Inner Liberation: A Pathway to Freedom — 31
12. Redefine Your Life Path by Re-Routing — 34
13. A Key to Success and Prosperity: Letting Go — 36

14	Blessings: The Language of Happiness	39
15	A Catalyst for Vibrant Health: Sunlight	41
16	Healing Past Trauma with Deep Breathing	44
17	Power of Love	47
18	Unleashed Your Inner Champion	49
19	Ignite Your Fire by Using Solitude, and Sensitivit	52
20	We are Either Getting Better or Getting Worse	55
21	The Unseen Battles: A Woman's Silent Struggles	57
22	Conclusions	60

Dedication

This book is dedicated to my father Dr. Nemichand P. Bafna, Mother Meena N. Bafna and daughter Manasvi G. Bohara.

Acknowledgement

It is my sincere gratitude to my spiritual teacher, life teachers, and all those who have crossed my life path and taught me many of the life's secret. They gave me tools that helped me to navigate my life journey smoothly.

I want to thank all my Gurus who made me a strong person in my life. They also helped me to shape my life knowingly or unknowingly.

Special thanks to my friends Hemsingh Patle and Manoj Sonawane for helping me to bring out this book from me and published it. They were instrumental in bringing out my story in sequence and also organized the tools and concepts of this book as per the need and order.

Preface

Dear Reader,

The world is filled with millions of books. But as a reader, you chose the title- Discover the Power of Your Emotions: Unlock the Strength from Within. My heart feels gratitude for you and I extend my sincerest thanks from the depths of my heart for being the instrument of change by reading it. The story of this book may connect you with me even if you are living a thousand miles away or never met me. It's a story about life, it's a story of survival, it's a story of a woman.

Some of the challenges I shared in this book will move you but I have to express it to go to the depth of my life story. If there is an emotional setback, then there is also a way to overcome it. This book addresses both emotional setbacks and triumphs.

As I bid farewell to you, I want you to know that we are the same at the level of universal consciousness but born with different stories. May my story inspire you to reach higher levels in your life.

With Warmth and Wisdom,
Dr. Snehal Jain

Foreword

It is an honour to write this foreword for the book "Discover the Power of Your Emotions: Unlock the Strength From Within by Dr. Snehal Jain". This deeply personal yet universally relevant book is a testament to resilience, transformation, and emotional strength. Life's journey is filled with unexpected challenges, and Dr. Snehal's story is one of overcoming adversity with courage. Through her experiences of love, loss, and self-discovery, she offers profound insights into emotional healing, self-worth, and the power of inner strength. Her narrative is not just about personal struggles but about rising above them with wisdom and grace.

What makes this book exceptional is its ability to inspire. It is a roadmap for anyone facing emotional setbacks, teaching how to turn pain into purpose. Dr. Snehal's emphasis on self-development, forgiveness, and emotional mastery is a powerful guide for those seeking growth.

Her journey reminds us that while life may shatter our illusions, it also provides opportunities to rebuild. This book encourages readers to embrace their struggles, find their inner resilience, and emerge stronger. It is a source of hope and empowerment for all.

I commend Dr. Snehal Jain for sharing her journey with such honesty and depth. May her story illuminate the path for many, reminding us that wisdom is born from experience and that transformation is always possible.

With admiration,
Dr. Oommen David

Book Review

This is a beautiful story of Dr. Snehal's grit and conviction. A testament to resilience, not giving up, and standing for your own self. The book just does not narrate a story, but gives people hope and faith that no challenges or difficulties in life are final, you can use whatever happens for your growth and development. My hope is that this book reaches the right people across the world and gives them the courage they may be searching for.

-By Avinash Anand Singh, India's Leading Growth Mindset & Peak Performance Coach

The book **Discover the Power of Your Emotions by Snehal Jain** is a courageous and heartfelt account of a woman who turned her struggles into strength. This book offers not just her story, but practical tools to navigate life's challenges. A rare and bold voice on relationships, essential reading for both women and men seeking to understand the emotional depth of a woman's journey.

- By Manoj Sonawane, author of the book Learning 2.0.

"**Discover the Power of Your Emotions**" is a raw and honest journey through emotional pain and healing. The author does an exceptional job connecting the dots between internal turmoil and external behaviors, especially in the context of how society too quickly labels people without recognizing the deeper pain beneath. A must-read for all.

-By Hemsingh Patle, author of the book The 5 Minutes Magical Habits

Reading **Discover the Power of Your Emotions** was a life-changing experience for me. Dr. Snehal Jain's honesty, courage, and spiritual wisdom shine through every page. Her journey from heartbreak and despair to strength and self-mastery inspired me to face my own struggles with renewed hope. This book doesn't just tell a story—it guides, heals, and uplifts. It's a true gift for anyone on a path of personal growth and emotional empowerment.

-By Dr. Swapnil Jawale, Dental Surgeon, TMD Specialist

After reading this book, each one of us feels the ups and downs of our own life story. It objectively evaluates human emotions, struggles and challenges and describes how those challenges were overcome with a smile and courage. Certainly, the author deserves praise for this beautiful and effective writing. We as authors best wish her a bright future.

-By Vimlendra Ranawat(RAS), Sub-division Magistrate, Pali

1

My Journey

****

"Sometimes it's the journey that teaches you a lot about your destination."
- Drake

I was born in a beautiful hill station Lonavala and brought up in the small village Vadgaon (Maval), near Pune, India. I lived my early years in a home that was made of thatched roof. At the time of my birth my dad had just completed his internship after MBBS from J.J. Hospital.

I was the youngest having one elder sister and one elder brother. My father worked very hard then and even today. In fact, today he is working harder than ever.

He started his practice in our village. I'm very lucky to have such inspiring and motivational parents as they are role models to me and many in our lives.

As days passed by, our financial status improved. They together built a big house for us, but one room at a time and by the time I was 8 years of age, we were living in a three storeyed building.

They brought the best for us as they could do for all three of us and also did the same for my cousins. They made all sacrifices.

We grew with the best food, facilities, comfort and lifestyle. I used to love singing, dancing and always desired to be the champion of all or all-rounder so that I can make my parents feel proud of me.

However, I was never selected in finals in any of the sports or activities. I started feeling I'm good for nothing. However, I was good at sports and this feeling made me a little bit happy. But unfortunately sports was underrated in the 1990s. I developed an inferiority complex. Had seen my parents struggling to build their life from scratch. So the value of every penny was huge for me.

I was a typical village girl with all big dreams and to my knowledge Mumbai was the city to make my dreams come true. I wanted to be a renowned Surgeon or say Red Carpet Celebrity in my chosen field and Mumbai was a world for me that would fulfill my life of dream, name, fame, and prosperity. As it is said it's a city that has a power to convert any dreams into reality.

I completed my Graduation in dental surgery and held my dream to be the queen of Mumbai and painted a picture of the perfect Prince in my life. Yes, I got married in 2009 to a person who was not less than a Prince in looks and his lifestyle, however life had many surprises wrapped for me. Soon in six months, I learned I was a mom-to-be. I felt blessed.

I had started my dental practice in my dad's hospital at Vadgaon. I traveled a lot from Mumbai to Vadgaon and back between 2009 to 2017.

My journey continued however, by the time I was in the second trimester, my husband was going through a massive financial crisis, and on the other hand I was gifted with a baby in my womb.

Soon I lost our home. I was at the lowest level of my life. I had only rupees 50 with me at that time.

Completely in shock, shattered and broke, I started staying with my parents at Vadgaon and my husband settled for some time in Rajasthan after this setback.

I didn't give up, as I knew I had a new life growing in my womb which was the best gift from God. Life continued, I was taken care of by my parents very well in the best possible way.

However, I was in depression, and had no presence of senses and thereby unable to understand the movements of my baby in the womb (which was very important to connect mother with baby).

I was constantly worried about losing my baby as well. As a baby was the only thing I had at that time. But somehow I overcame this period. The day came and I was gifted with an Angel. I had spent all my gestational period in stress and anxiety. The day when she was born, my husband came just to see her for a couple of hours and left immediately and never came for the next 6 months. I continued my practice soon after my C- section (Cesarean) as I had understood, that my daughter is my responsibility now.

Life has to move on, no matter how big challenges it throws on you, you have to overcome it or let's make it more light with this line "As if the universe conspires the problems for you to make you more strong". It was just the beginning of my problems. This was also a moment for me when I saw the light from within.

The key point on Emotions:

Despite heartbreak, financial crisis, and the pain of abandonment, a mother's love and responsibility becomes a guiding force, that transforms despair into determination. Thus, emotions, when channeled with purpose (here mother's love and responsibility for daughter), have the power to rebuild even the most shattered dreams.

2

Don't Let Love Blind you

****
"Sometimes when you lose your way, you find yourself."
- Unknown

On the 17th of April 2009, I got married. In the quiet darkness of that fateful night, as I lay on the cold, unforgiving carpet, I couldn't help but reflect upon the choices that had led me to this moment. The stars outside seemed to mock the tears that welled up in my eyes, glistening like unspoken dreams. My heart, once overflowing with hope, was now drowning in the reality of my decisions.

Before the bond was officially accepted, the man I thought was my soulmate put in immense effort to convince me that he was the perfect partner. I believed his words and trusted him completely, only to find myself on my wedding night in a crowded room, sleeping on a rough carpet next to a washroom amidst a sea of strangers. The special moment every girl dreams of was shattered, but I swallowed my heartbreak with a forced smile.

I wish I had recognized the initial signs of being taken for granted, of being completely fooled by my innocent trust. Even on the very next day, my father, sensing my distress, urged me to reconsider, offering to help me find someone more deserving. I dismissed his plea, thinking that things would improve, or that someday my dreams of a happy marriage would come true. But that day never arrived. Instead, my life became a cycle of unending work, responsibility, and silent tears. There were no celebrations, no festivals, just the monotony of a loveless existence. I was trapped in a marriage devoid of joy, imprisoned by my own blindness and deafness to the harsh realities of my situation.

I had placed my trust, my faith, in a love that was blind. Blind to the warnings whispered by my parents, who had weathered life's storms and knew the difference between love and infatuation. They had sensed the hollow promises, the empty words that had woven a web around my vulnerable heart. Yet, in my youthful naivety, I had chosen to ignore their wisdom, believing in the power of love to conquer all.

There was the icy distance that had grown between us. The mangalsutra, a symbol of our sacred bond, lay forgotten, a stark reminder of unfulfilled vows. How could I have missed the signs? How could I have ignored the truth that was laid bare before me? My parents, in their silent suffering, had known all along.

As I write this, tears flow, not just for my own pain but for the countless others girls who might fall into the same trap. My hope is that by sharing my story, I can make you aware of the dangers of blind trust. Don't let the promises of others deceive you until you truly understand their character. Spend time with them, know them inside out, and most important don't overlook the warning signs.

I made a vow to myself - a vow to never let emotions cloud my judgment again. I pledged to be practical, to listen to the voices of experience that had guided generations before me. Blind love,

I understood now, was a treacherous path, leading only to regret and heartache.

I found the strength to rise from that sour relationship, leaving behind the shattered illusions of my blind love. I vowed to rebuild my life, not on the foundation of blind faith, but on the pillars of wisdom, discernment, and the unwavering support of my family.

It's a cautionary story, a proof to the importance of heeding the advice of those who have walked the path before us. Let us not be blinded by the illusion of love, but instead, let us open your eyes to the reality of the relationships you choose. In the embrace of practicality and the guidance of experienced hearts, you find the true essence of love – a love that stands the test of time, a love that weathers every storm, and a love that is built on a foundation of trust, respect, and unwavering devotion.

Let's learn how to rebuild the shattered life in the next chapter.

The key point on Emotions:

Blind emotions, especially in love, can cloud judgment and lead to deep regret. Trusting blindly without discerning a person's true character can result in heartbreak and suffering. True love is not just about feelings; it must be built on wisdom, practicality, and mutual respect to stand the test of time.

3

Building Dreams Against All Odds

****

"Be Your Own Light."
- Buddha

As my daughter approached her second birthday, the weight of responsibility of her future bore down upon me. My world had narrowed down to this precious little soul, for my husband and the man who was supposed to be her father had no interest in our well-being. The burden of ensuring her education and future fell squarely on my shoulders.

Despite my humble background and lack of knowledge about the ways of the world, I resolved to give my daughter the life she deserved. Armed with nothing but a mere fifty thousand in June 2012, I embarked on a journey into the unknown. Determination and love fueled my desire to create a better life for us, even in the face of complete despair.

In my quest to provide her with the best, I sought the help of strangers, navigating the complexities of school admissions and finding a property to lease for my clinic. I was ignorant, but my resolve was unyielding. I was determined to build the life of my dreams without relying on anyone else. With sheer determination, I managed to secure admission for my daughter in the best playgroup available and leased a 250-square-foot area for my clinic.

Though I had no idea how I would manage financially, I started working on the interiors of my clinic. Despite my broken spirit, I took pride in creating a top-notch, advanced clinic, a testament to my unwavering dedication. Even today, in 2023, visitors commend the quality of my clinic, a validation of my relentless efforts.

My journey became a balancing act between my hometown Vadgaon Maval, where I practiced dentistry every Friday night to Sunday night, and Dombivli (a suburb near Mumbai) from Monday morning to Friday evening, where I managed cooking, my daughter's schooling and the clinic. I was determined to build a future for us, and my parents offered their support in every way they could. Yet, I yearned to stand on my own two feet.

In April 2013, I made the difficult decision to entrust my daughter's care to my mother. This sacrifice allowed me to focus on honing my skills, building my practice, and ensuring a stable future for my daughter and me. I was laying the foundation for a future that was built on my terms.

In the next chapter, let's discuss how to use the path of self-development to overcome any challenge.

Key point on Emotions:

Powerful emotions, when channeled with purpose, can transform adversity into strength and create a foundation for a better life.

4

Unlock the Strength from Within

****

"Feelings are something you have; not something you are."
- Shannon L. Alder

In the span of 11 years, from 2006 to 2017, I embarked on an intensive journey of self-investment. Every course, every certification, every skill I pursued it all, driven by the belief that success was synonymous with professional accolades, big names, and hefty paychecks. From one-day practice management courses to year-long business management programs, from mastering dental techniques like crowns, bridges, veneers, and dental implants to diving into the intricacies of facial aesthetics and orthodontics, I did it all. Yet, despite my extensive expertise, there was an emptiness within me, a void that couldn't be filled by professional accomplishments alone.

It was a moment with my coach, Dr. Manish Chitnis, that became the turning point. He pointed me toward a different path, one that led inward. I enrolled in Landmark, a transformative self-development program. Little did I know that this decision would shake the very core of my being.

During a Landmark workshop, I experienced a panic attack so severe that I had to be taken home by my family members. This incident brought forth the stark reality of my mental health struggles. I had battled with thoughts of suicide, attempting to end my life multiple times, seeking an escape from the overwhelming pain that life had dealt me.

The 5th of September 2018 stands as a haunting reminder. On that day, I reached the edge, attempting to end my pain in the most tragic way. It was my daughter who witnessed my anguish, her innocent eyes reflecting the fear and confusion. I realized the profound impact my actions had on her, and that awareness stopped me in my tracks. Even in that darkest moment, I understood that ending my life wasn't the solution. I realized that no one but my father and my daughter truly cared about my existence.

With this epiphany, a newfound determination blossomed within me. I decided to confront the grief of my failed relationship head-on. I chose to build resilience, to master my emotions, and to find strength in the face of adversity. It was a daunting journey, one that demanded unwavering courage and self-acceptance. I started to unravel the layers of my emotions, embracing them instead of succumbing to them. I sought therapy, understanding that seeking help is a sign of strength, not weakness.

I learned this profound truth: The journey of mastering your emotions is a testament to your resilience and your capacity for growth. Your emotions control your physiology. The place, the people, the smell, the random memory are enough to trigger your emotions and that decides your state of mind. Learn to control it (emotions). The feeling (happy or sad) experienced by you are the product of your emotions. If you observe it consciously, then you'll find that you are slave of your emotions and they decide your mood and it changes constantly throughout a day or let's simplify it in this line "your cues decide your mood". I was the person who was trap in bad emotions of my failed relationship which I was experiencing repeatedly. This single emotion was enough to kill me and my dream. It was draining my energy and were making me a hollow person from inside. When I understood this truth, I stop feeding to this emotion and over the time I weaken its root. Today, I accept the emotions that serve my purpose and growth. As a human I experience both happy and sad emotions but learned which to keep for me. The sad emotions are like passing waves of sea water that is going to fall on sea shore but will move back.

This journey of mastering my emotions is ongoing. It's a daily practice, a continuous commitment to my own well-being. I've come to realize that true success isn't just about external achievements; it's about the internal battles we face and conquer. It's about finding the strength to rise after every fall, to face our darkest demons, and to emerge stronger, wiser, and more compassionate.

In sharing this deeply personal chapter of my life, I hope to inspire others who might be facing similar struggles. I want you to know that you are not alone, that there is strength within you even in your weakest moments. As you read my story, I urge you to reflect on your own journey, your own struggles, and to find the courage to seek help, to confront your inner battles, and to emerge victorious.

I am not only investing time and money on my self-development but also committed to staying at the forefront of my field, constantly learning and evolving to offer the latest and most effective techniques. Whether it's a subtle enhancement or a complete smile makeover, my goal is to create results that are not only beautiful but also harmonious with the individual's overall facial structure.

Through my practice, I've had the privilege of witnessing incredible transformations – not just in appearance but also in the way my patients carry themselves, with newfound poise and self-assurance. It's a profound joy to be able to contribute to their journey toward enhanced confidence and self-love.

Your body is like whole system. The error at one place triggers to the other. I experienced it hard way in my life. Let's learn about it in the detail in next chapter.

Key point on Emotions:

Know your inner feelings and learn to conquer on them. Take the time to explore and comprehend the depth of your inner emotions thoroughly, as this understanding is crucial for personal growth. Once you have attained a clearer insight into how you feel, make it a priority to implement the necessary actions that will enable you to effectively gain control over those emotions and master them in a way that serves your overall well-being.

5

Resilience in the Face of Adversity

****

"If an egg is broken by an outside force, life ends. If broken by an inside force, life begins. Great things always begin from the inside."
- Jim Kwik

December 15, 2019, marked a pivotal moment in my life, a day that thrust me into a world of uncertainty and fear. I received the shocking diagnosis of a 2kg growth in my abdomen, a silent intruder that had gone unnoticed within me for two long years. Just two days later, on December 17, 2019, I found myself on the operating table in my hometown, Vadgaon, undergoing surgery under general anesthesia. As I emerged from the anesthesia-induced haze, the words that greeted me were sharp and piercing: "Tu zinda hai?" ("Are you alive?")

Those words shattered my already fragile state of mind. Nights turned into endless hours of sleeplessness, plagued by the overwhelming weight of my health concerns and the future that lay ahead. On one hand, I grappled with the uncertainty of my own well-being, and on the other, my heart ached for my young daughter who faced the world alone, studying in the 5th standard without her mother by her side. I was broken, completely and utterly, drowning in loneliness and despair.

I survived and was discharged from the hospital with a list of medicines. In an attempt to divert my mind from the constant overthinking, I turned to the solace of an activity I had always found comfort in cooking. With each culinary creation, I found a temporary escape, a way to channel my emotions into something tangible and nourishing, especially when it was for my beloved Dad, who had always been my pillar of strength.

Days passed, and I made the journey to Dombivli, where my daughter awaited me. On January 18, 2020, I resumed my work at the clinic, determined to regain a sense of normalcy amidst the chaos that had engulfed my life. Little did I know that another storm was brewing on the horizon – the lockdown brought about by the global pandemic.

As the world came to a standstill, I found myself sinking deeper into a victim mentality. Questions of "Why me?" echoed in my mind, as if the universe had conspired against me, dealing blow after blow. Yet, amidst the despair, a glimmer of strength began to emerge. It was a resilience that had been buried deep within me, waiting for the right moment to surface.

My spirit was tested during this chapter of my life. It was a journey through the darkest corridors of fear and despair, but it was also a journey toward resilience, hope, and ultimately, triumph. In the face of adversity, I discovered a reservoir of inner strength, a strength that would carry me through the challenges that lay ahead and transformed me into a beacon of inspiration for others who found themselves navigating similar storms. Little did I know, this phase of my life would become the foundation upon which I would rebuild myself, emerging stronger, wiser, and more compassionate than ever before.

You find the solution when you decide to get to the root of your problem. It's like things would be given to you when you ask for it. I received it in the form of morning rituals. Let's learn how it helped me in the next chapters.

The key point on emotions:

Make sure that you don't let any emotions interfere with your process of healing. It's important to maintain a firm guard against those feelings that could distract you from your path to recovery.

6

Despair to Discovery

****
"Ask for help. Not because you are weak. But because you want to remain strong."
- Less Brown

Amidst the eerie silence of a world in lockdown, my own turmoil continued. The separation from my daughter, the physical and emotional aftermath of surgery, and the relentless questions that haunted my nights created a storm within me. I questioned my existence, wondering why life had chosen to burden me so profoundly.

In the midst of this darkness, I embarked on a seemingly ordinary day, March 22, 2020, with an extraordinary determination. Despite my weakened state and against the advice of rest, I attempted a 110-kilometer journey on my bike to Vadgaon. Yet, reality struck hard; my body, still healing, couldn't bear the strain. I had to retreat, the distance too vast for my fragile strength.

As I lay there, contemplating my limitations, I realized that the physical pain from the surgery was dwarfed by the emotional burden I carried. Each night, the haunting question echoed in my mind: "Why me?" Desperation led me to prayer, a plea to the universe for guidance, for a revelation of purpose in my suffering.

In the midst of this despair, a ray of hope emerged in the form of Amol Karale's workshop. With newfound determination, I embraced a morning routine, a ritual that became my sanctuary. In the quiet moments of those mornings, I discovered a reservoir of strength within me, a resilience that whispered of my capacity to overcome.

It was during these introspective mornings that I met the hidden creative content writer within me. With a newfound purpose, I confronted my weaknesses and fears head-on. I refused to let my vulnerabilities hold me hostage in the clutches of victimhood. On March 28, 2020, my transformation journey took a definitive step forward.

With a heart fueled by newfound courage, I embarked on my action plan. I started to pen down my thoughts, my struggles, and my triumphs. Writing became my catharsis, a channel for the emotions that had long been suppressed. In embracing my creative side, I found solace. Each word I wrote, each fear I faced, was a step away from the victim I once was and toward the empowered, resilient individual I was becoming.

Amidst despair, I found the strength to not only endure but to rise. The journey from despair to discovery was marked by pain, yes, but it was also illuminated by the spark of resilience within me. Little did I know that this newfound strength would become the driving force behind my transformation, propelling me toward a future I had never dared to dream of. The journey was far from over, but now, armed with self-discovery and determination, I faced the challenges ahead with newfound courage and a sense of purpose.

This phase of my life led me to discover more secrets of the universe. I came to know about the Law of Karma. We abide the laws of our country or city in the same way we have to abide the Law of Karma that governs our universe. Let's learn about it in the next chapter.

The key point on emotions:

Emotions can empower you to overcome any challenge, as they arise from within. As we know from the ages that one has to win the life battle from inside rather than outside. No matter how many kilometers you travel, you'll still feel strength because of this internal power.

7

Why Me? Karma and Fate

****

"What goes around comes back around again."
- *Grand Puba*

In the depths of despair, I questioned why life's burdens fell upon me, and the answer whispered through the cosmic winds: the world is but a mirror. We attract what we are, and what we send forth echoes back to us. I decided to understand the subtle threads of karma that bind us in this universe.

The Invisible Threads of Karma

Let me take you back to a time when I stood at a crossroads, grappling with life's uncertainties. It was then that I stumbled upon the profound concept of karma. Like you, I was intrigued by its mystery. But as I delved deeper, I realized that it's not just a philosophy; it's a guiding force shaping our destinies. Each action, thought, and emotion is intricately intertwined with the universe, echoing through time. Whether you believe in the Law of Karma or not, but I can tell you from my experience that it has shaken my life and I have paid some Karmic debt in this lifetime and prayed to God many times to reduce it in this life.

My life transformed when I embraced the Karmic laws. The power of intention, the echo of our actions, and the harmony of the universe—it all became clear. By aligning my actions with positivity and compassion, I witnessed miracles unfold. I reduced the impact of Karma by implementing acts like donations, showing kindness to fellow humans, love to animals and Mother Earth, and blessed the people who helped me in my life journey.

The hatred and negativity for others build your Karmic debt. I am grateful to God that he made me aware about this law in this lifetime. I realized that understanding this law isn't just wisdom; it's a transformative tool that empowers us to shape our reality, one thought at a time that is devoid of any hatred and negativity and I am conscious of it now. It seemed that God had thrown challenges at me to awaken me from a deep slumber.

The next key thing I learned in my life was forgiveness. If the law of karma binds you with other person through your act, then forgiveness is the key that separates your identity from that person and help you declutter your life. Forgive a person who hurt or humiliated you. The forgiveness works like an unbinding agent because you get separated from that person's energy. What's the use of that thoughts and emotions that drains your energy? better let it go. I have paid the price for holding the emotions of hurt. Let's learn how in the next chapter.

The key point on emotions:

Emotional balance is nothing but the Karma balance. Some in-depth emotions are like past karmic energy and impact your present feelings because that want to rationalize the things of your life.

8

Forgiveness: A Path to Spiritual Liberation

****

"Reading is to the mind what exercise is to the body and prayer is to the soul."
*- **Matthew Kelly***

On that fateful Tuesday morning of April 19, 2022, when the world was waking up to a new day, I woke up to darkness in my left eye. It was as if the universe had dimmed a part of my sight, urging me to seek clarity within myself. This incident became a profound moment of reflection, a stark reminder of the fragility of life and the importance of inner healing.

In the depths of my confusion, my coach appeared as a guiding light, leading me toward a transformative path. With his wisdom, I embraced the power of forgiveness, a concept that transcends the boundaries of human understanding and taps into the very essence of our spiritual being.

I embarked on a soul-stirring journey of forgiveness, writing letters to my past, my loved ones, and even to myself. Each word penned down was a step toward spiritual liberation, a sacred act that released the burden of resentment and opened the doors to profound inner peace.

Through this experience, I discovered the spiritual significance of forgiveness. It wasn't just about letting go; it was a profound act of self-love and acceptance. It was a recognition of our interconnectedness with the universe, acknowledging that harboring grudges and pain hinders our spiritual growth.

There may be millions of reasons against your partner but learn to forgive him/her. No matter how sharp arrow your partner throws at your heart. Remove the arrow and heal your heart, otherwise, it is going to take a toll on you because a bleeding heart spreads the poison in whole body. The ignorance and casualness of my partner led me into casualty and I have already shared this experience in the earlier chapter.

The things didn't move in life until you have a growth mindset and know your money well. That's the reason I decided to invest in both the mindset and finance aspects of my life. Let's discuss about it in the next chapter.

The key point on emotions:

Forgive and move—that's the medicine for an emotional breakdown. The longer the duration, the deeper the pain. Just take a moment to imagine the significant impact that can occur if you choose to carry that emotional pain for an extended period of time. It can weigh heavily on your spirit and mind, affecting your overall well-being. It is crucial to actively release those feelings before they start to take a toll on your physical body. By letting go of emotional burdens, you can prevent them from manifesting in harmful ways, allowing yourself to heal and find peace.

9

The Mirror Effect: Harnessing the Power Within

****

"All the power is within you! And all you have to do is take it out."
- Mehmet Muraildan

I stumbled upon a profound truth: the world around us is merely a reflection of our inner selves. It was a revelation that transformed my perspective, making me realize the immense power I held within my thoughts, my actions, and my beliefs.

I delved into the intricate web of the law of attraction, understanding that we attract into our lives what we emit from within. Our thoughts, the food we consume, and the energy we radiate all play a significant role in shaping our reality. With this newfound wisdom, I embarked on a remarkable journey of self-discovery and transformation.

I made a conscious decision to invest all I had earned into my own growth. I sought out mentors and coaches who could guide me in mastering the art of abundance, money, and manifestation. Ron Malhotra became my mentor in mastering money mantras, Kartika Nair illuminated the path of the Law of Attraction and Manifestation, and Ameet Parekh shared invaluable insights on business management. Each course, each interaction, even the ones that seemed like wrong decisions at the time, became stepping stones in my personal and professional growth.

However, the turning point arrived when I made a significant investment in my own well-being by having a life coach and mentor, Avinash Anand Singh. His guidance was a beacon of light, illuminating my path toward self-mastery and resilience. They say that when the student is ready, the teacher appears. I had reached a point in my life where I was receptive to change, and Avinash became the catalyst for my transformation.

I am deeply grateful for each mentor I crossed paths with, for their wisdom, guidance, and unwavering support. Their influence shaped my journey, and my gratitude knows no bounds.

From the year 2020, my focus shifted entirely. I became resolute in my determination to build myself stronger, to face every adversity and challenge as an opportunity for growth. Instead of retaliating when faced with negativity, I chose a different path. I embraced the metaphorical stones thrown at me not with bitterness, but with resilience. I refused to stoop to the level of those who tried to bring me down. Instead, I chose to respond with kindness and generosity, offering the fruits of my knowledge and experience.

For I realized, when people throw stones at you, it's because they see something valuable in you – like a tree laden with ripe fruits. Instead of engaging in a battle of negativity, I chose to inspire change. By sharing the seeds of my own transformation, I hoped to inspire others to alter their life paths, to embrace positivity, and to find their own strength within. This philosophy became the cornerstone of my resilience, empowering me to face life's challenges with grace and fortitude.

This chapter of my life was not just about self-discovery; it is a proof to the transformative power of positivity, gratitude, and self-investment. The lessons I learned enabled me to face every challenge with a positive attitude, and every setback was a stepping stone toward a brighter, more empowered future.

Now, in the next few chapters, I will share various tools and concepts that helped me to triumph my life journey. They came to my aid and shattered my hollow illusion and transformed myself from a person who was blind in love with a person, then was trapped in her own thoughts and life problems and finally metamorphosed herself into a person of complete wisdom.

The key point on emotions:

The urge for change is an emotional bet. It drives us from within. This intuition works like a compass and connects you with the right people. Make sure you be compassionate with this compass.

10

Harnessing the Energy of Abundance

****

"If you want to find the secrets of the Universe, think in terms of energy, frequency and vibration."
- ***Nikola Tesla***

In the depths of my journey, I discovered the profound impact our thoughts and energy hold on our lives. I grasped the truth that our thoughts are not merely fleeting ideas; they are potent energy, capable of shaping our reality. It was a revelation that changed the way I perceived the world and my place within it.

One of the most transformative lessons I learned was that money, too, is energy. It's not just paper and coins; it's a powerful force that flows through the universe, responding to the energy we emit. Understanding this fundamental truth allowed me to redefine my relationship with money. I realized that my financial reality was a reflection of my energetic vibration, my thoughts, beliefs, and emotions about money.

However, the true essence of abundance was unveiled to me through my life coach. With his guidance, I delved into the depths of what abundance truly means. It's not merely about monetary wealth; it's a state of being, a mindset of plenty. It's the understanding that the universe is limitless in its offerings, and our thoughts and energy are the magnets that attract this limitless abundance into our lives.

Under the training of my coach, I harnessed the power of channelizing my energy effectively. I learned to align my thoughts, beliefs, and emotions with my desires. I discovered the art of manifestation – the ability to transform my thoughts into tangible reality. It was a revelation that I held within me the power to create my own destiny, to shape my financial reality, and to achieve my goals beyond my wildest dreams.

In a moment that felt like magic, I achieved my monthly earning goal in just one day. It was an evidence to the trust my coach had in me, a belief that surpassed my own self-confidence. He saw the power of manifestation within me, even when I doubted myself. It was a powerful lesson that belief in oneself, coupled with the focused channeling of energy, could yield extraordinary results.

The ability to channelize energy is a tremendous gift we all possess. It's a force that can transform our lives, our circumstances, and our reality. The key lies in our hands – how effectively and purposefully we choose to use this energy. By aligning our thoughts, beliefs, and actions with our desires, we unlock the infinite power within us, ushering in abundance, success, and fulfillment.

This chapter of my life was a profound exploration of the limitless potential residing within every one of us. It was a reminder that our thoughts and energy are not just abstract concepts but tangible forces that shape our destiny. With this understanding, I embraced the power within me, shaping a future that was not just abundant in financial wealth but rich in fulfillment, purpose, and boundless possibilities.

In the next chapter, we'll learn about inner liberation by using the 10-step process.

The key point on emotions:

Emotions are a vital part of your energetic vibration and play a crucial role in shaping your reality. They are not just fleeting feelings but powerful forces that influence your thoughts, beliefs, and actions. By aligning your emotions with your desires and maintaining a positive, abundant mindset, you can effectively channel your energy to manifest your goals and attract limitless abundance into your life. Money is just one part of this process.

11

Inner Liberation: A Pathway to Freedom

****

"Only you can take inner freedom away from yourself, or give it to yourself. Nobody else can."
- **Michael A. Singer**

Amidst the chaos of everyday life, there lies the profound quest for inner liberation. This chapter is a guide, illuminating the transformative steps toward finding tranquility within, unveiling the soul's freedom from the shackles of negativity and self-doubt. Let's awaken your inner freedom with these 10 steps.

1. Self-Reflection and Awareness:
Cultivate mindfulness. Reflect on your thoughts, emotions, and reactions. Awareness is the first step towards inner freedom.

2. Acceptance and Letting Go:
Embrace your flaws and past mistakes. Letting go of self-judgment liberates the soul. Acceptance is the doorway to peace.

3. Forgiveness:

Release the burden of grudges. Forgiving others and yourself heals wounds, allowing love and compassion to flow freely.

4. Practice Gratitude:

Cultivate gratitude for life's blessings, big and small. Gratitude shifts focus from lack to abundance and foster inner contentment.

5. Meditation and Mindfulness:

Dedicate time to meditation. Quieten the mind, and connect with your inner self. Mindfulness anchors you to the present moment and dissolves any anxiety.

6. Nurture Self-Compassion:

Treat yourself with kindness. Be your own best friend. Self-compassion nurtures resilience and cultivates your positive self-image.

7. Embrace Impermanence:

Understand that change is constant. Embracing impermanence allows you to flow with life. It also reduces resistance and inner turmoil.

8. Cultivate Authentic Relationships:

Surround yourself with positive, supportive individuals. Authentic connections uplift you. It nurtures your spirit and sense of belonging.

9. Pursue Passion and Creativity:

Engage in activities that bring you joy. Pursue hobbies and creativity. Passion fuels the soul and provides an outlet for self-expression.

10. Seek Inner Guidance:

Connect with your intuition. Listen to your inner voice. Trust your instincts. They are pathways to inner wisdom and liberation.

In the pursuit of inner liberation, remember: it is not a destination but a continuous journey. Each step taken, no matter how small, brings you closer to the profound freedom that resides within. Embrace this journey with open arms, and you will discover the boundless peace and serenity that lie at the core of your being.

In the next chapter let's learn about "re-routing" a word that is famous by Google Maps. It also has a profound meaning behind it.

The key point on emotions:

Emotions are deeply intertwined with inner liberation. By cultivating 10 step process, you can transform negative emotions into sources of strength and peace. Letting go of grudges, embracing gratitude, and staying mindful help you release emotional burdens, allowing you to experience true freedom and tranquility within.

12

Redefine Your Life Path by Re-Routing

****

"It is pointless to embark on any journey if you do not believe yourself worthy of the destination."
- Anthon St. Maarten

Have you noticed how Google Maps never yells, condemns or castigates you if you take the wrong turn? It never raises its voice and says, "You were supposed to go left, at the last crossing, you idiot! Now you're going to have to go the long way around and it's going to take you so much more time, and you're going to be late for your meeting! Learn to pay attention and listen to my instructions, OK!?"

If it did that, chances are, a lot of us might stop using it. But Google simply Re-Routes and shows you the next best way to get there. Its primary interest is in getting you to reach your goal, not in making you feel bad for having made a mistake.

There's a great lesson here. It's tempting to unload our frustration and anger on those who have made a mistake (by taking the long route), especially those who are close to us. But the wisest choice is to help in fixing the problem (by finding the new best route or re-routing), and not to blame. Let's Introspect and know when did I and you had Re-Routing moments recently. That might have helped you redefine your life path gracefully. The final aim of re-routing is to reach your destination (goal) and not to blame and yell on others.

"Re-routing" helps you get to the desired place whereas the "Art of Letting Go" creates a new path for you. Let's learn how to do this in the next chapter.

The key point on emotions:

Emotions like frustration and anger can cloud judgment and harm relationships, especially when mistakes occur. Instead of reacting with blame or criticism, adopting a calm, solution-focused approach—like "re-routing"—helps maintain harmony and guides others (or yourself) toward the goal. By prioritizing problem-solving over emotional outbursts, you foster understanding, resilience, and progress, ultimately leading to a more graceful and effective path forward.

13

A Key to Success and Prosperity: Letting Go

****

"If you want to fly, you have to give up what weighs you down."
- Roy T. Bennett

This chapter discusses the concept of letting go and it's one of the key to create prosperity and success in your life. It's a profound practice deeply rooted in the principles of healing, guiding you to release the burdens that hold you back and embrace the path to success with open arms.

Understanding the Illusion: In our quest for prosperity, we often cling to illusions, blinded by attachments and expectations. The journey of letting go begins with recognizing these illusions and understanding that true prosperity lies in freedom, not in the chains of attachment.

The Essence of Healing:
Drawing wisdom from the teachings of healing, we learn that energy is the key to our well-being. By releasing stagnant and neg-

ative energies through the art of letting go, we create space for abundance to flow effortlessly into our lives. Here is step-by-step guide to letting go it gracefully:

1. Awareness: Begin by becoming aware of the emotions and attachments that weigh you down. Acknowledge them without judgment.

2. Breath of Life: Practice deep, conscious breathing to cleanse your energy. Inhale positivity, exhale negativity.

3. Forgiveness: Release the grip of resentment by forgiving yourself and others. Forgiveness is a powerful tool for healing.

4. Detoxify Your Space: Just as we cleanse our bodies, it's essential to purify our living and working spaces. Remove clutter and create an environment that fosters positive energy.

5. Energy Cord Cutting: In Pranic Healing, cutting energetic cords with people or situations that drain your energy is a liberating practice. Visualize the cords dissolving, setting you free.

6. Gratitude Journaling: Cultivate an attitude of gratitude. Regularly jot down the things you are thankful for. This simple act shifts your focus from lack to abundance.

7. Meditation and Visualization: Engage in daily meditation to calm the mind. Visualize yourself letting go of burdens and welcoming prosperity into your life.

Blessings Through Letting Go:

As you embark on this journey of releasing the old and making room for the new, remember that letting go is not a loss but a gain. Blessings unfold when we open our hearts and hands, allowing life to flow naturally.

A Beautiful Message for You:

In the garden of life, the art of letting go is the gentle breeze that carries away the old leaves, making way for new blossoms. May you find the strength to release, the courage to embrace change, and the wisdom to recognize the abundant blessings that follow.

May your journey be filled with light, love, and the serenity that comes from gracefully letting go.

Let's learn about the importance of blessings in the next chapter.

The key point on emotions:

Emotions, when left unaddressed, can become heavy burdens that block prosperity and success. By practicing seven-step process, you can release negative emotions and energetic attachments, creating space for positivity and abundance to flow into your life. Letting go of emotional weight is a transformative act of healing, allowing you to move forward with clarity, peace, and openness to new opportunities.

14

Blessings: The Language of Happiness

****

"There's a blessing in everything that happens to us."
- Kamaru Usman

Despite the pain, I choose to bless each person in this journey. Their presence, and their actions, have carved the path toward my wisdom and strength. In their roles as messengers of God, they made me wiser, resilient, and unyielding. I hold deep gratitude for the lessons they brought, knowing that each experience was a blessing in disguise. I used the following blessing prayers to amplify happiness and shower the love for the people around me.

Wishing Love and Healing Prayers:

"May love find its way into their hearts, joy illuminate their days, and healing mend the wounds that may lie within. I wish them prosperity, abundance, and success, but above all, wisdom to guide them in every step. May they always be at their best, equipped with the strength to face life's challenges".

Blessing is the language of happiness. It amplifies love for others. It's divine in nature. It will heal you faster than any other medicine in the world.

In the next chapter, let's learn about the healing power of sunlight. As we know emotions trigger sad feelings that in turn cause depression. The person is unable to come out of it if she experiences it repeatedly. Those in this situation prefer to live in a dark room or place. The impact of the depression can be reduced if we show the sunlight to that person.

The key point on emotions:

Emotions like pain and resentment can be transformed through the act of blessing and gratitude. By choosing to bless those who have caused pain, you shift from negativity to love and healing. This practice not only fosters emotional resilience and wisdom but also amplifies happiness and inner peace, allowing you to grow stronger and more compassionate through life's challenges. Blessing others becomes a divine act of self-healing and empowerment.

15

A Catalyst for Vibrant Health: Sunlight

****

"The wound is the place where the Light enters you."
- Rumi

In our daily lives, one essential thread often overlooked is the gentle touch of sunlight. Beyond its warmth and brightness, sunlight holds an astonishing power – the ability to influence our internal environment profoundly. Embracing the sun bath ritual not only illuminates our external world but also rejuvenates our internal clockwork, playing a pivotal role in maintaining our circadian rhythm.

The Circadian Symphony: Nature's Harmonious Rhythm
Our bodies dance to the rhythm of the sun, following a natural circadian rhythm that regulates sleep, hormone production, and overall vitality. Exposure to sunlight, particularly in the early morning, sets the tone for our biological clock. It signals the brain

to produce serotonin, the 'feel-good' hormone, promoting a sense of well-being and alertness.

Sunlight: The Key to Revitalization

As we know sunlight triggers the synthesis of vitamin D, often referred to as the 'sunshine vitamin.' This vital nutrient is a linchpin in bolstering our immune system, promoting bone health, and enhancing overall cognitive function. By basking in the sun's glow, we not only replenish our vitamin D levels but also uplift our mood and energy levels.

Elevating Abilities and Actions

A harmonious circadian rhythm, orchestrated by regular sun exposure, optimizes our body's internal environment. It enhances our ability to focus, elevates cognitive functions, and sharpens our reflexes. When our internal clock is finely tuned, our actions become more purposeful, our decisions more precise, and our creativity flows effortlessly.

Contributing to Overall Wellness

The sun bath ritual is a cornerstone of holistic wellness. It cleanses not only our bodies but also our minds and spirits. The soothing warmth of sunlight alleviates stress and anxiety, promoting mental clarity and emotional balance. As our internal environment harmonizes, our resilience strengthens, enabling us to navigate life's challenges with grace and poise.

The significance of sun baths cannot be overstated. It weaves a thread of vitality, connecting us to the natural rhythms of the universe. So, let us embrace the sun's gift with open arms, allowing its radiant energy to transform our internal landscape, revitalizing our abilities, actions, and ultimately, our entire being.

Let's learn how to heal past traumas by using the breathing exercise in the next chapter.

The key point on emotions:

Sunlight has a profound impact on emotional well-being by boosting serotonin production, the "feel-good" hormone. Regular exposure to sunlight, especially in the morning, uplifts mood, reduces stress and anxiety, and promotes mental clarity and emotional balance. By aligning with the natural circadian rhythm, sunlight helps create a harmonious internal environment, fostering resilience and a positive emotional state.

16

Healing Past Trauma with Deep Breathing

✷✷✷✷✷✷✷✷

"As soon as healing takes place, go out and heal somebody else."
- **Maya Angelou**

In the intricate dance between mind and body, the science of deep breathing emerges as a fascinating and powerful tool, especially in the context of healing past traumas. Let's demystify the science and delve into practical, intriguing techniques that can transform your journey to recovery.

1. Understanding the Science

At its core, deep breathing activates the parasympathetic nervous system, the body's natural relaxation response. When you take slow, deliberate breaths, your brain signals the body to release calming neurotransmitters, like GABA, which alleviate anxiety and stress. Additionally, deep breathing enhances blood flow, ensuring optimal oxygen supply to your organs, promoting a sense of clarity and focus.

2. The 4-7-8 Technique: A Breath of Serenity

One of the most effective techniques is the 4-7-8 breathing method. Inhale quietly through your nose for a count of 4, hold your breath for 7 counts, and then exhale audibly through your mouth for 8 counts. This technique not only relaxes your nervous system but also encourages a sense of control and tranquility.

3. Diaphragmatic Breathing: Cultivating Resilience

Practice diaphragmatic breathing by placing one hand on your chest and the other on your abdomen. Inhale deeply through your nose, allowing your diaphragm to expand fully. Feel your lungs and abdomen fill with air. Exhale slowly, releasing all tension. This technique not only calms your mind but also strengthens your diaphragm, enhancing your lung capacity and overall well-being.

4. Visualization: Guiding Your Breath

Combine deep breathing with visualization. Imagine your breath as a golden light, entering your body with each inhalation, dissolving past traumas and negative emotions. As you exhale, visualize dark clouds of pain leaving your body. This technique not only engages your senses but also empowers your mind to actively participate in the healing process.

5. Rhythmic Breathing: Harmonizing Body and Mind

Experiment with rhythmic breathing by matching your breath to a calming rhythm or sound, like ocean waves or a gentle heartbeat. Sync your inhalations and exhalations to this rhythm, allowing your body and mind to align with the soothing pattern. This technique not only promotes relaxation but also cultivates a profound sense of harmony within.

By embracing these practical and scientifically grounded techniques, you empower yourself to navigate the intricate pathways of healing. The art of deep breathing becomes not just a practice but a fascinating exploration of the profound connection between your breath, your body, and your ability to heal from within.

The key point on emotions:

Deep breathing is a powerful tool for regulating and healing emotions, particularly those tied to past traumas. By activating the parasympathetic nervous system, deep breathing reduces stress and anxiety, promoting calmness and emotional balance. Techniques like the 4-7-8 method, diaphragmatic breathing, and visualization help release negative emotions, fostering resilience and a sense of inner peace. Through these practices, you can transform emotional pain into healing and clarity.

17

Power of Love

****

"Love is the vibration of spirit and song of the universe."
- Unknown

In the vast realm of emotions, falling in love is effortless, but the true challenge lies in rising in love. Love, a word so powerful, should never be tainted. As I write this, my earnest plea echoes: build yourself, connect with the higher power, and embrace a love that brings only joy, not pain. These three steps can help you harness the power of love.

1. Self-Building and Empowerment:
Invest in your own growth, both mentally and emotionally. Strengthen your core which in turn forms the foundation of enduring love. When you are grounded in self-love, you become a powerhouse of positivity, radiating strength that attracts genuine connections.

2. Hold onto Love that Uplifts:
Love should never cause pain or doubts. Choose a love that uplifts your spirit, a love that stays, unwavering and constant. Do not settle for being an option in someone's life; demand respect and priority. The love you deserve is one that nurtures, respects, and cherishes you.

3. The Power of Positive Vibration:
Your energy, your frequency, shapes the love that comes your way. Cultivate positivity, and you will draw a soulmate whose vibrations align perfectly with yours. In this harmonious connection, infidelity finds no room; trust and loyalty become the foundation of your relationship.

It's natural that we fall in love with a person without knowing him well. But believe me, we get attracted to the soulmate based on our vibration. A person of high life value will be attracted to a person of the same vibrations. Also, one who deceives others will also be deceived by others, a trustworthy person attracts a trustworthy person into their life. Build a high-value life by adopting truthfulness, higher ethics, and integrity.

The Key point on emotions:

Love is a powerful emotion that should uplift and empower, not cause pain or doubt. By cultivating self-love, aligning with positive vibrations, and choosing relationships that nurture and respect you, you can create a harmonious and fulfilling connection. Your emotional energy and life values shape the love you attract, making it essential to build a high-value life grounded in integrity, truthfulness, and positivity.

18

Unleashed Your Inner Champion

****

"The only person you are destined to become is the person you decide to be."
- Ralph Waldo Emerson

You are not merely a part of this universe; you are a universe in its entirety, teeming with potential, dreams, and limitless capabilities. Within you lies the power to overcome, to thrive, and to sculpt your destiny. The following five-step process may help you to unleash your true potential.

1. Embracing Self-Compassion:
Your journey begins with the gentle embrace of self-compassion. Acknowledge your flaws, your fears, and your imperfections. Even in vulnerabilities, you can find the raw materials for your growth. All you need to do is treat yourself with kindness, and infinitely worthy.

2. The Strength in Self-Belief:

Believe in your dreams with a fervor that sets your soul ablaze. Your belief is not just a whisper; it's a roaring thunder, shattering doubts and illuminating the path ahead. With unwavering faith in your abilities, you can conquer mountains, because there is no limit to your potential.

3. Turning Challenges into Triumphs:

Life's challenges are not roadblocks; they are stepping stones to greatness. Embrace adversity as a teacher, guiding you toward resilience. Every setback is a setup for a comeback. With tenacity and self-belief, you can turn every trial into a triumph, emerging stronger and more resilient than before.

4. Embodying Self-Reliance:

Self-reliance is not about isolation; it's about the empowering art of self-trust. Trust your instincts, your intuition, and your inner wisdom. Your heart and mind are your greatest allies, guiding you toward decisions that align with your authentic self. Rely on your inner compass; it will never lead you astray.

5. Celebrating Self-Accomplishments:

Acknowledge your achievements, no matter how small they seem. Each step, each victory, is a testament to your strength and perseverance. Celebrate your progress; it's a reminder of the incredible journey you are on. Your accomplishments, no matter how minor, pave the way for monumental victories.

We have unveiled many profound truths of life in this book, embrace them. Even the small changes are enough to shift the orbit of your life.

Key point on emotions:

Emotions like self-compassion, self-belief, and resilience are the driving forces behind unlocking your true potential. By embracing self-compassion, you transform vulnerabilities into strengths. Self-belief fuels your dreams and helps you overcome challenges, while resilience turns setbacks into opportunities for growth. Trusting your inner wisdom and celebrating your accomplishments further empowers you, creating a positive emotional foundation for achieving greatness.

19

Ignite Your Fire by Using Solitude, and Sensitivit

****

"Fire is the test of gold; adversity, of strong men."
- *Martha Graham*

The solitude and sensitivity are two keys that can help you to ignite the fire within you. It's like you are holding the power to transform despair into a burning desire and that in turn fuels the extraordinary legacy.

Embrace Solitude, Embrace Self:
Solitude becomes your sanctuary, a sacred space where the whispers of the higher power find their way to your soul. Here, in the quiet moments, you discover the answers you seek. Take the time to listen, for within the silence, you find the guidance needed to shape your destiny. It helps you get a clear vision of your life. Amidst the constant doubters and naysayers, your belief in

yourself and your dreams becomes your armor. You are not just a daydreamer; you are a visionary, capable of weaving the fabric of reality with the threads of your imagination. Visualize yourself in your dreams that will help you create a blueprint of your future.

The Unseen Strength of Sensitivity:

Sensitivity is not weakness; it's a superpower. It fuels your empathy, your creativity, and your ability to connect deeply with others. Let your sensitivity be the force that propels you forward. You have a limit as you can't do all the things by yourself. Visualize your goals and allow your intuition to work in your favor. You'll find the right person that in turn will help you to accomplish your goals. For example, my book manuscript was ready and I was looking for the person to help me in editing, proofreading, and bringing the flow in my book and the person appeared in my life who not only accomplished all the above work but also helped me to get this book published.

Know that your sensitivity is your strength, your emotions your driving force. Embrace the unknown faces, for they bring opportunities to be your authentic self. Your dreams are not mere illusions; they are the seeds of your legacy. Ignite that burning fire within, and let it guide you to heights unimaginable. You are not just a daydreamer; you are the architect of your destiny, creating a legacy that will echo through generations. Embrace your power; you are unstoppable.

The key point on emotions:

Sensitivity fuels empathy, creativity, and deep connections, while solitude allows you to connect with your inner self and higher guidance. By embracing these emotions, you can turn despair into desire, visualize your dreams, and attract the right people and opportunities to help you achieve your goals.

20

We are Either Getting Better or Getting Worse

****

"Life is a dynamic game. We are either getting better or we are getting worse."
- David Goggins

Most of us have experienced this truth of life many times- "Either you get better or life is going to make you worse". Life favors those who continuously strive for growth and adapt to change. Life will love you if you give her better input. I was the person who was spirally going down but decided to bounce back. I experienced my growth once I accepted the path of transformation (change).

There will always be chaos around us but it's you who make the things in order. Take the decision, seek help, and move to the next level of life. Not all things will work in your favor. I had a dream of a better life after the marriage but it didn't work. I accepted this as my failure and moved on from it. I would not have survived, if I had denied this reality (by getting stuck in the past and a failed relationship). I rebuild my life on the foundation of spirituality. It's a path that most people lack in our society. I forgive my husband; I bless the people who come across my path. I pray for the well-being of others. Had I not embraced these changes in my life, I may have remained stuck in my past behaviors.

Things take shape when we realize our mistakes. I wrote the first page of this book when I lost everything. Your inner self comes out when nothing is left for you. That's the beauty of life. It wants us to drop the ego, it wants us to be grounded, it wants us to be more human in nature.

In all the above chapters, I have shared my life story, concepts, and tools in this book. I decided to add this social aspect of a woman's life in the last chapter. A woman faces a lot of hurdles and criticism when she faces the life path single-handedly. It is an unseen battle and she encounters it every day. Let's learn it in the next chapter.

The key point on emotions:

Emotions like acceptance, forgiveness, and resilience are essential for personal growth and transformation. By embracing change, letting go of past failures, and grounding yourself in spirituality, you can rise above chaos and rebuild your life. Accepting reality, forgiving others, and focusing on self-improvement allow you to move forward with grace and strength, turning life's challenges into opportunities for growth and deeper humanity.

21

The Unseen Battles: A Woman's Silent Struggles

****

"There is nothing stronger than a broken woman who has rebuilt herself."
*- **Hannah Gadsby***

A woman often fights battles that remain hidden from the world. Behind her resilient smile lies chaos, a personal turmoil that society conveniently overlooks. Speaking out seems impossible; every avenue is riddled with judgment and prejudice. Following are some of the social aspects she deals with on a daily basis.

The Deafening Silence:
Her lips remain sealed, burdened by the fear of judgment. To share her pain means risking the wildfire of gossip that spreads like a pandemic. Society, quick to label and criticize, forces her

into a suffocating silence, where her cries for help echo in the hollows of her heart, unheard and unnoticed.

The Invisible Weight of Societal Norms:
In this unforgiving environment, even sharing her struggles with fellow women invites scrutiny. What should be a moment of empathy transforms into a storm of rumors, leaving her more isolated than before. Turning to men for solace becomes a perilous venture, misconstrued as an invitation rather than a plea for understanding.

The Veiled Tears and Sleepless Nights:
As night approaches, her pillow and the solitude of the bathroom become her confidants. There, hidden from the world, she releases the tears that society doesn't allow her to shed openly. The strength that holds her together during the day shatters in these moments, revealing the immense weight she carries.

Judgment: The Uninvited Guest:
The sad truth is, even without understanding her plight, people assume the roles of judges and advisors. They offer unsolicited opinions, dissecting her character without a hint of authenticity.

The Authenticity of Empathy:
In a world quick to criticize and slow to understand, what she truly craves is authenticity. A genuine, empathetic ear that listens without judgment. A heart that understands the unspoken words, offering solace without questioning her integrity.

The Anxiety and Depression:

A person suffering from anxiety and depression feels alone even when she is surrounded by others. Often, she feels chaotic and becomes sad unintentionally. She cannot make anyone understand or make sense of this emptiness and loneliness. She also doesn't know what's wrong with her. Let's not crush such weak souls around us. They are what they are because of some reason.

Let us recognize the silent battles fought by the women around us. Let us be the listeners without prejudice, the shoulders without judgment, and the voices that uplift rather than condemn. For in understanding her struggles, lies the path to a more compassionate, understanding society, where the strength of a woman is celebrated, not questioned, and her silent tears are acknowledged, not ignored.

The key point on emotions:

Women often endure profound emotional pain in silence due to societal judgment and lack of empathy. Their struggles with anxiety, depression, and loneliness are compounded by the fear of being misunderstood or criticized. What they truly need is authentic empathy, a safe space to express their emotions without judgment, and compassionate support to help them navigate their battles. Recognizing and addressing these silent struggles is essential to build a more understanding and compassionate society.

22

Conclusions

****

"There is no real ending. It's just the place where you stop the story."
*- **Frank Herbert***

In the quiet shadows of my life, where despair threatened to consume my very soul, I was a woman whose spirit radiated a kind of quiet courage that can move any rock from the path of my success. I was not just a single mother; I was an unwavering love, the embodiment of strength in vulnerability. The world, however, didn't see my resilience. Instead, some men saw my softness as an opportunity, my kindness as a weakness, and my helplessness as an invitation to exploit.

Imagine for a moment the pain etched on my face as I navigated a world that had turned its back on me. Yet, within the confines of my heart, I harbored love, gratitude, forgiveness, and blessings for all the people who came across my path. Every night, as I kissed my child goodnight, my eyes spoke volumes of the battles I fought silently, shielding my little one from the harsh realities that threatened to shatter our world.

The conclusion part of this book is the narrative of a single mother who endured such trials because life became a difficult journey for them (single mothers) until they decided to make a change and overcome all the challenges in their life. This is the reason I wrote this book and shared my story with you. This book not only discusses different concepts and tools but also helps you to overcome life's challenges. Like me, there are many women out there who still need help, and this book may provide them with the guidance they need to overcome their life challenges.

Let this book be a testament to rewrite the narrative for every single mother and help them to turn their struggles into stories of hope, their tears into pearls of wisdom, and their despair into a symphony of unyielding strength.

www.ingramcontent.com/pod-product-compliance
Lightning Source LLC
LaVergne TN
LVHW010608070526
838199LV00063BA/5111